SUNFLOWER HUNT

poems

JOYCE WINSLOW

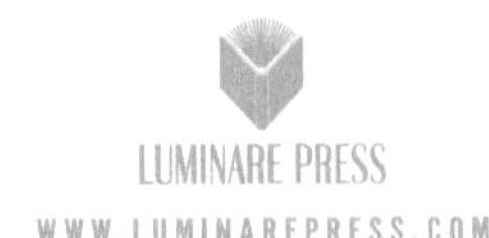

LUMINARE PRESS

WWW.LUMINAREPRESS.COM

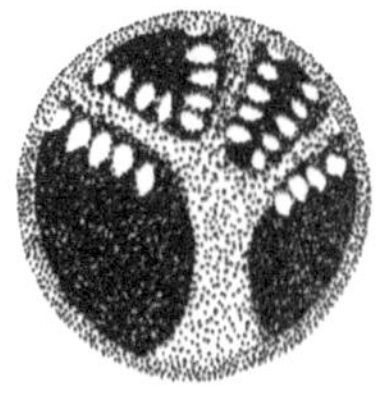

For Evan and Alison

Sunflower Hunt

You went searching sunflowers,
Sure of the ripe bloom,
Certain that with its seeds
You could sow the sun.

You expected a field of brilliance
At the end of the road:
A place to roll, a solitude,
An end.

O and there were sunflowers,
And some in the shapes you had supposed.
And there was a field, but it held
Thistles too, and lonely grasses ---

Blooms unnamed... colors untried
There was a field, but there was no
End of the road. Instead was a cloud
To draw you,

Promising no place and no thing,
Taking you beyond sunflowers
And beyond fields. . .
But how could you know, how could you know?

Genesis II

That day in the park
Our thoughts took shape
And formed a man,

Molding him in their likeness,
Good and bad.

Then came afternoon with a man-forgetting mist,
And our thoughts were gulls
That traveled out beyond our gaze,

Devoured by fog. After they had passed
There was only an emptiness of sky and sea, and
We awoke to silence with the faint memory

Of a sound like wings.

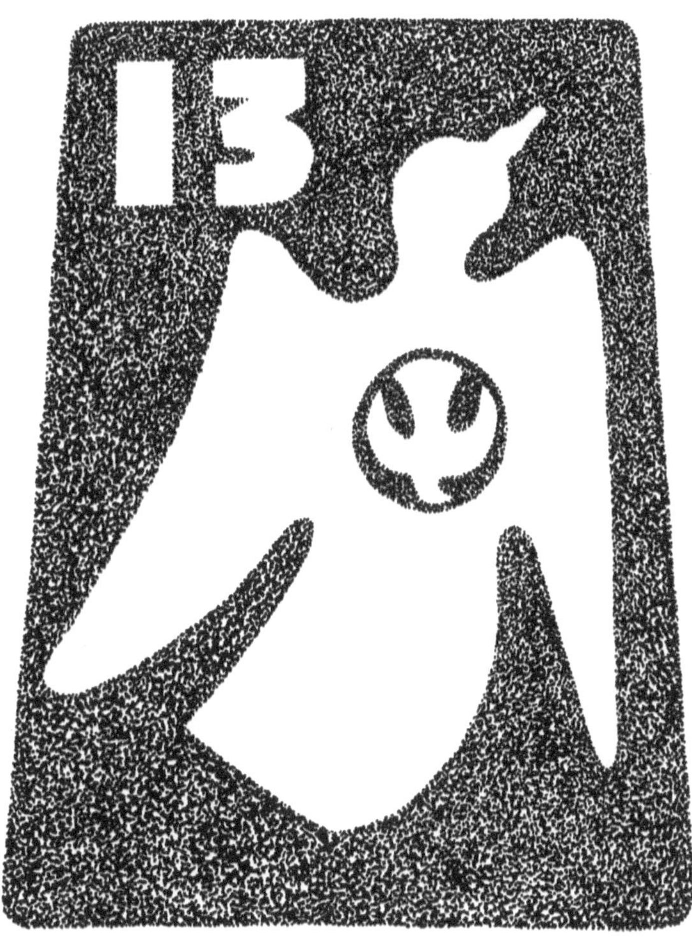

13

Learning Patience By Evening Light

The day went out the way it came,
Still fresh and faintly flushed, passing
Unhurried over the damp grass

As if nothing had happened and nothing
Needed to happen,
A day complete, seeking no meaning
For itself,
Coming on endlessly
Like a desert flower, opening and closing,
Closing and opening. . .

And we could imagine that the
Enormous white cat
Roused from sleep by our morning walk
Was settling again in its favorite chair
To await the magic of the moon.

Day Of The Cat

Hush . . .
The dry hills wait for rain,
Tautly quiet, quiet as the taut black
Cat in the golden weeds.

The dying light on the yucca plant proclaims:
This is the day of the cat, these hills are
His domain. The brittle shrubs, the marbled clay,
Have felt his passing.

We have felt his passing, passing through us
As through the silent grasses, tall on
The hills. We have moved with him and heard the
Occasional pebble stir,

Aware only of our catlike selves
In an eternal catlike moment.

Perhaps we wondered once if the yucca knew
That the clouds were pink and gray
And low over the hills,
But that was all.

Reflections After A Fire

The houses that we build
Must burn.
And brick we loved too well
Must suffer, scorch, and burrow
In the earth before the blaze;
The wind will scatter what we held
Like ash, the flames will raze
The earth, and torture trees,

And though we cry for justice
Our justice is that lizards appropriate
What remains,
Sleeping on fragmented steps
Which show the way we came.

From wasteland to wasteland
We must move, and build anew,
Until the last allegiance to our own
Is dead,
And we can hold within our hand
The one, the invincible stone.

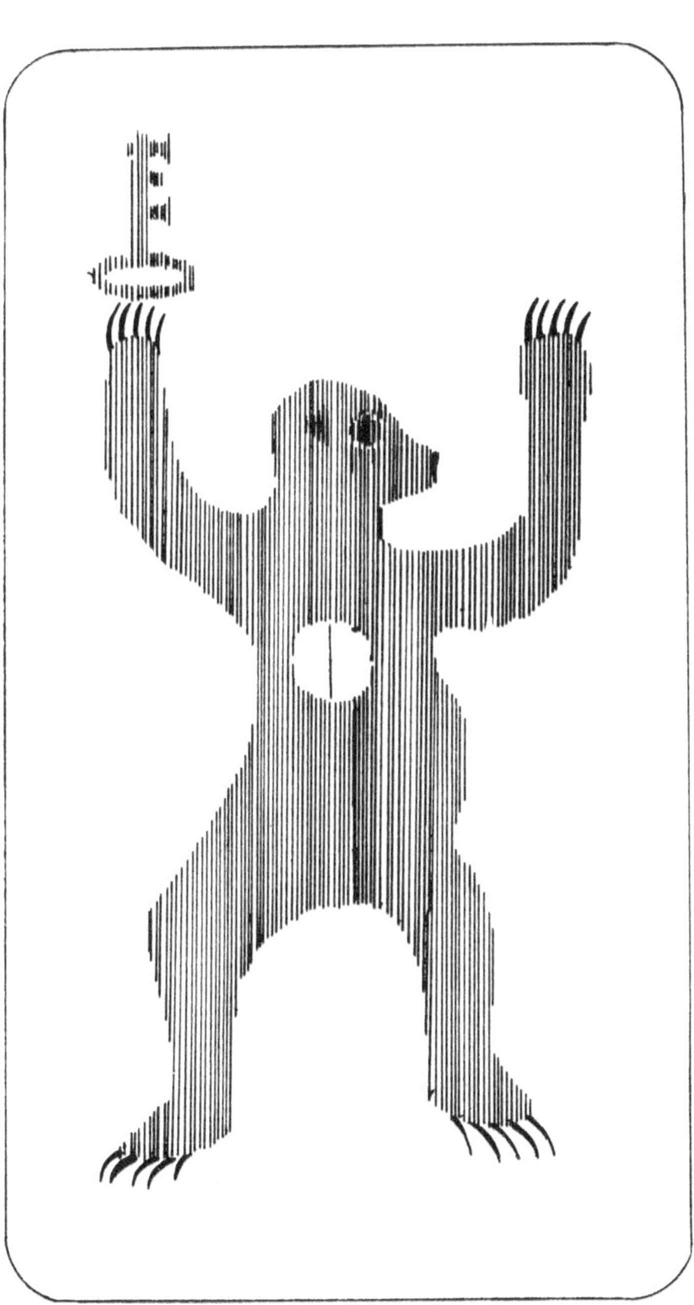

The Memories Of An Imagined Boy

Remember how it was to become invisible
By the lake, lying long in the grass
While summer buzzed about you - - -
And how you discovered yourself as the sky,

An uninhibited vapor, a blue seeping,
The veriest blue world. . .?

It was the same with the fog off Russian
Gulch when you, the kindest gray
Swallowing mist, imbibed the sea
And all its raggedness,

Imbibed the horizon
And yourself.

Someone wished, once, for a desert
To stand in alone, a desert to enter
And free the heart, letting it widen
Far and far, embracing the numberless sand.

To Certain Friends

At the first meeting,
You were as clear and fresh and free
As the center of rain.

Knowing nothing of you,
I knew everything.

Now that you have become a habit,
Assumed a shape and revealed to me
That shape's rough edges, the lie of flaws,

It seems I knew you best
Before I knew you well.

Ceremony

Each day when the sun goes out,
Spending its last radiance on that highest hill,
The gnats come to dance in the white waning light,
To spin a frenzied celebration

In the air, in the brilliant eye of the sun.
They are like atoms whirling, like
Exploded sun-fragments, like the world beginning
Again in silence, in the loneliest place.

The sky goes gray. A bird cries
One note from a thicket, remembering.
Slowly a large beetle crosses the rocks
Into the circle where the light was,

And the world is emptied again for night.

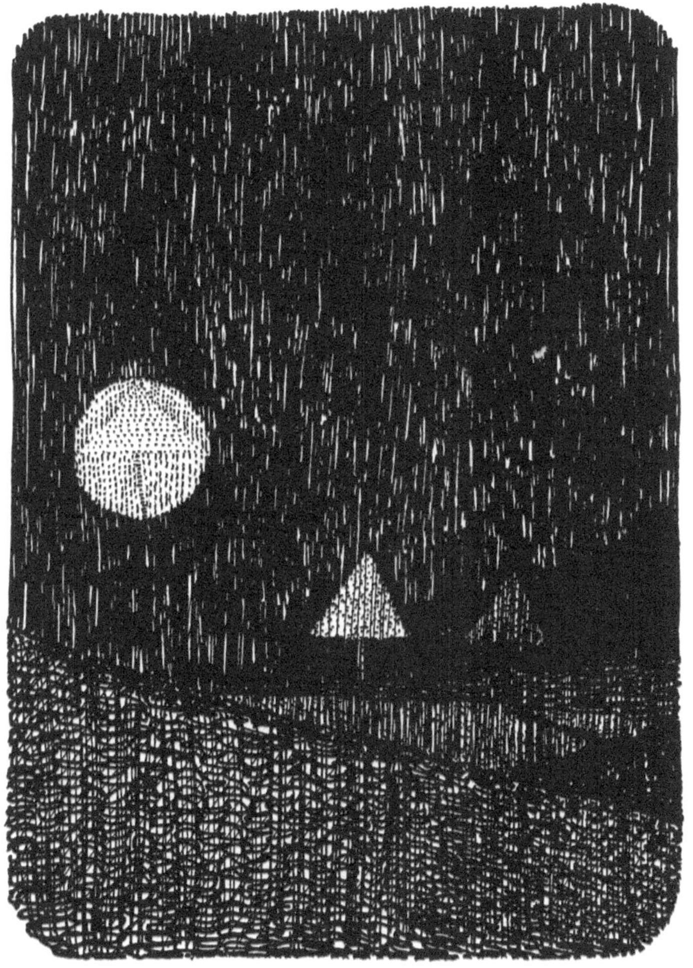

In Driftwood

It is ourselves we love,
And though we long to taste the sun,
Our paths are crooked, wound around:
Light slips away, and
Mornings find us on the beach, alone.

Oceans come, with salt for wounds;
We become
Shapes of their choosing
And we meet the sun
The hard way, blistering in sand.

We are made bones again, blanched, weightless,
Bared for life again:
Out of our pits and hollows spring small plants
And flowers - - -
For those occasional beachcombers,
A silent proud affirmation of green.

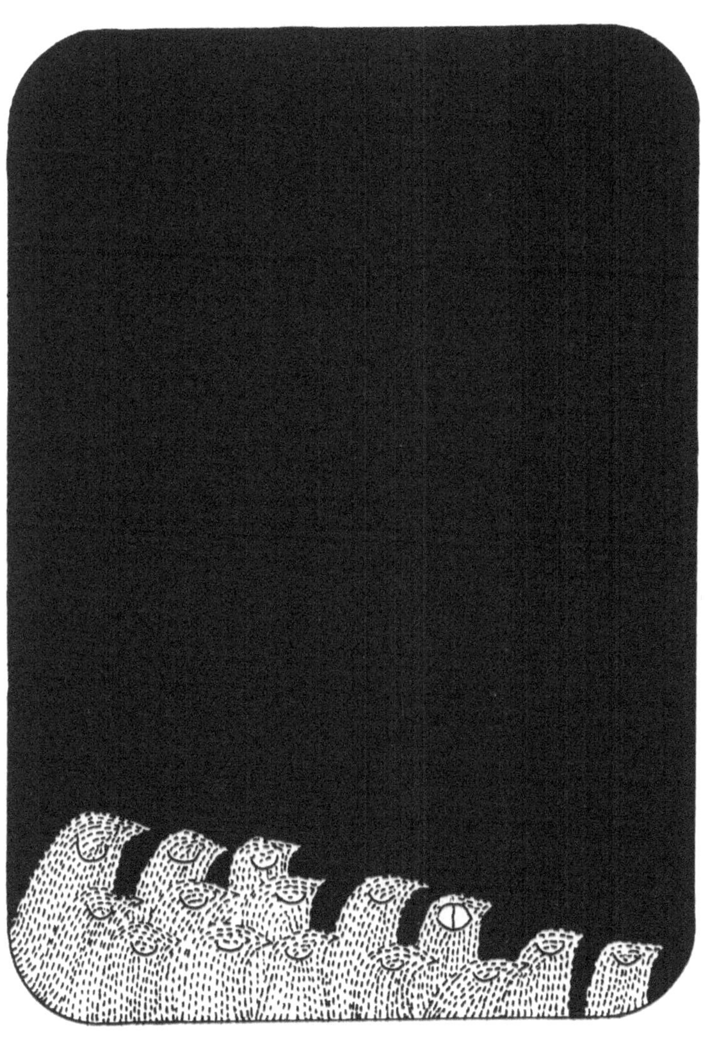

Jon, This Time. . .

Jon, this time you were new
To me as the surprises of the sky
And friendship was like the cloud
That formed from nothing,
A confident wisp in the evanescent blue:

The breath of love made visible,
Which borrowed from the infinity of sky
To teach the wondrous spaciousness
Of you.

For A Child Who Likes To Be Followed By The Moon

This morning the sun was a ball of tricks:
It leaped up from behind trees
Without warning, without prefatory
Violets or pinks or reds.

It socked us with a merry yellow - - - Pow!
Before we had a chance to think,
And made us wobbly with delight.

We thought perhaps that
You decided to be the sun today,
And proclaimed the world be governed by Surprise.

To A Bird Like Ourselves

What was it like to sit on the edge
Of the nest all night, looking out
Beyond darkness and beyond stars,
Waiting out the endless moment

Until dawn?
And what did you find to trust,
There on the edge of emptiness, with
The dark wind ruffling your feeble, untried wings?

I would like to know - - -
Did the sun burst like a revelation on the hill?
Did you see the whole morning at once,
And did some spirit embrace and free your heart,
So that you could leave. . . accepting the unknown?

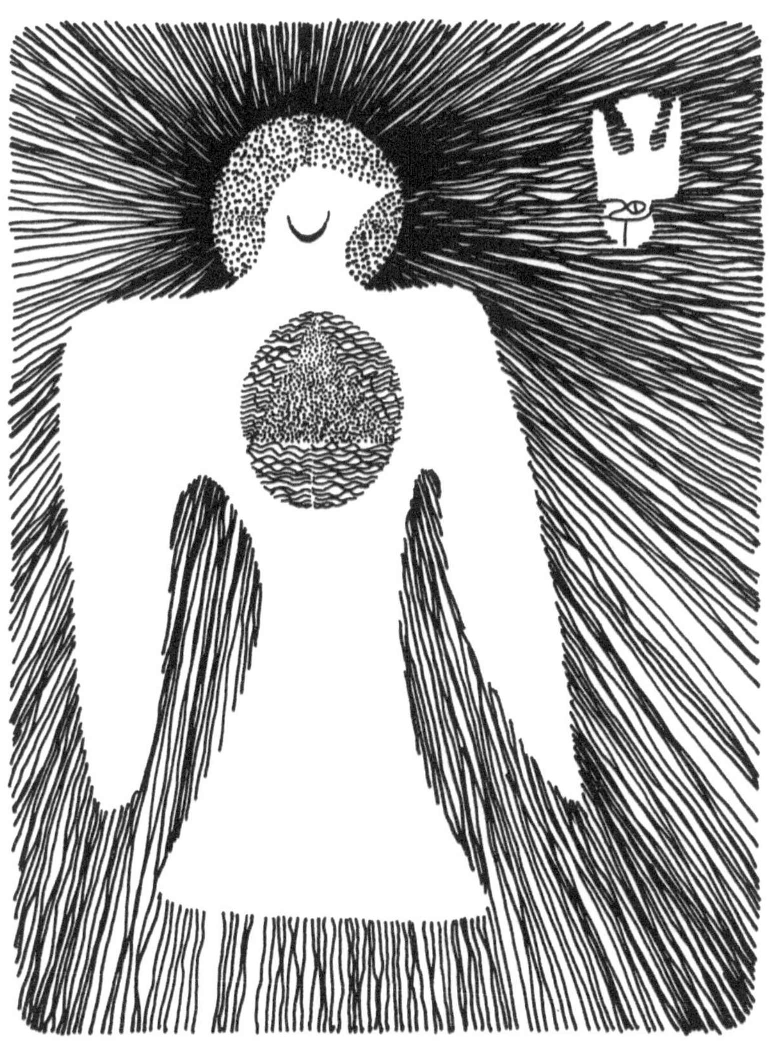

Once On A Day Continually Being Born

Once on a day continually being born
I beheld a sunlight, like music, on the leaves,
And watched how oaks and sycamores interpreted
Their ballet.

And if there had been a listening rain
I would have spoken then, saying,
Cleanse me of myself, o rain,
O quiet. Let me be an ear to hear that
Music, let me be the instrument on which

A music's played.

Thank You, Ann

It is bouquets we think of at times like these:
Blossoms from night's chalk garden, whitely permanent,
Brimming over the porcelain basin of the moon.
Or the moon itself as pussy-willow, gathered
In multiple images for your vase.
We think of dawn's red tulip and the chrysanthemum
Sun, and of the imperishable bloom of love.

We Learn From Trees

We learn from trees. . .
Love, anonymous among the leaves,
Has effaced their names.

Their silence tells their joy,
Whose tongues are borrowed from a breeze.
They live unannounced.

And when the boiling sky
Hurls out a wind to flay the world,
They bend. . . because they Know.

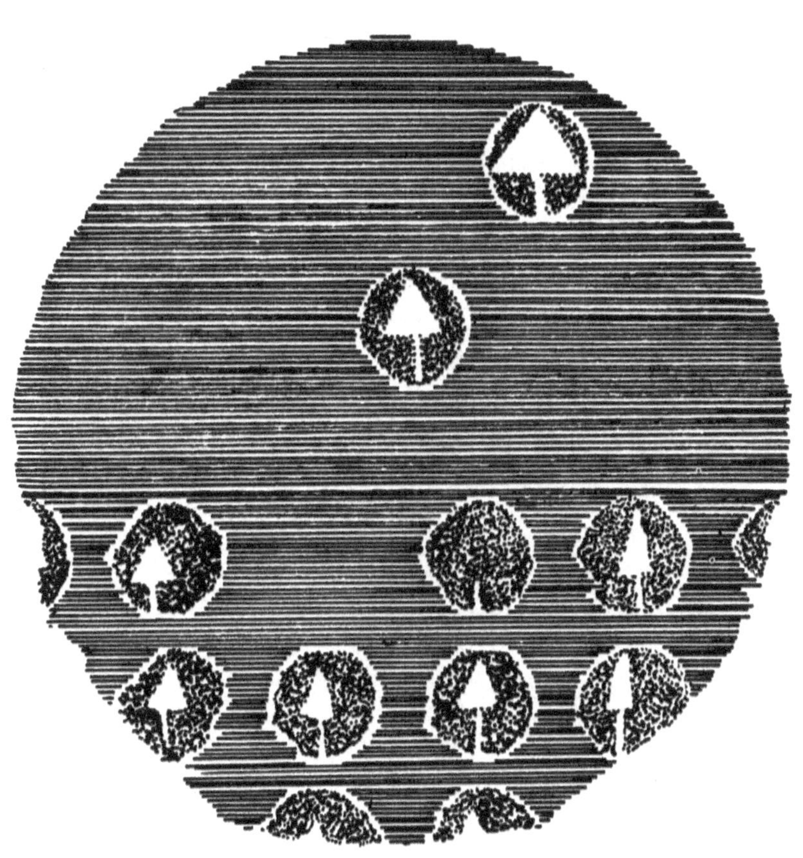

Thank You, Sibelius

You called me by a living name
And it echoed from the ceiling of the sky,
It bounded from the earth, ringing,
Careening - - -

a kind of allelujah.

I was that name, I lived
At the center of it while it zoomed,
And in that zooming moment you divested me
Of body, giving me instead

a Sound.

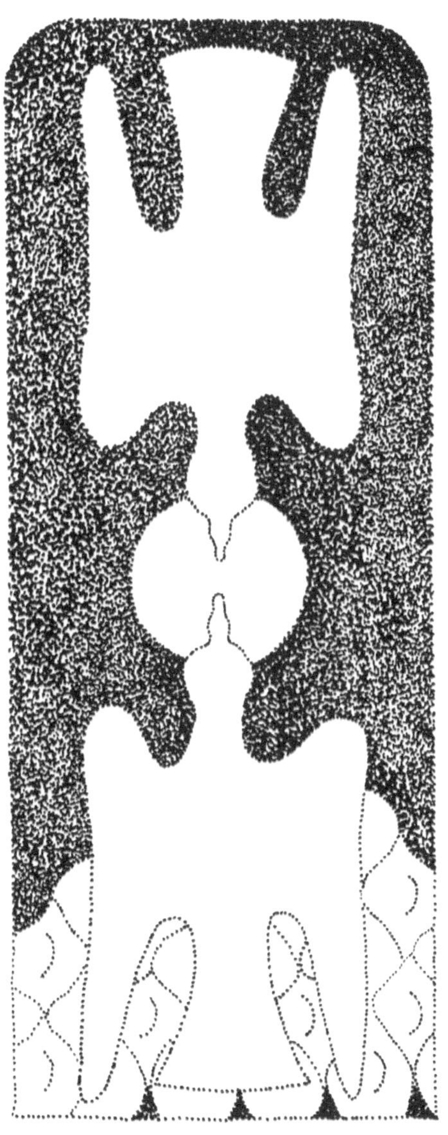

She Is The Poem

She is the poem, and summer is her white dress.
Around her, and yet still her,
The yellow afternoon; the trumpeting greens
Of the park, the deliquescent sky and
Distant bay, the blooms. . .

Close your eyes and encompass the moment
With your mind, how she laughs on the back
Of the marble camel guarding the museum, the
Camel from Prince Kao's tomb. And how

The very noon laughs, green and yellow,
To see her riding ancient death.

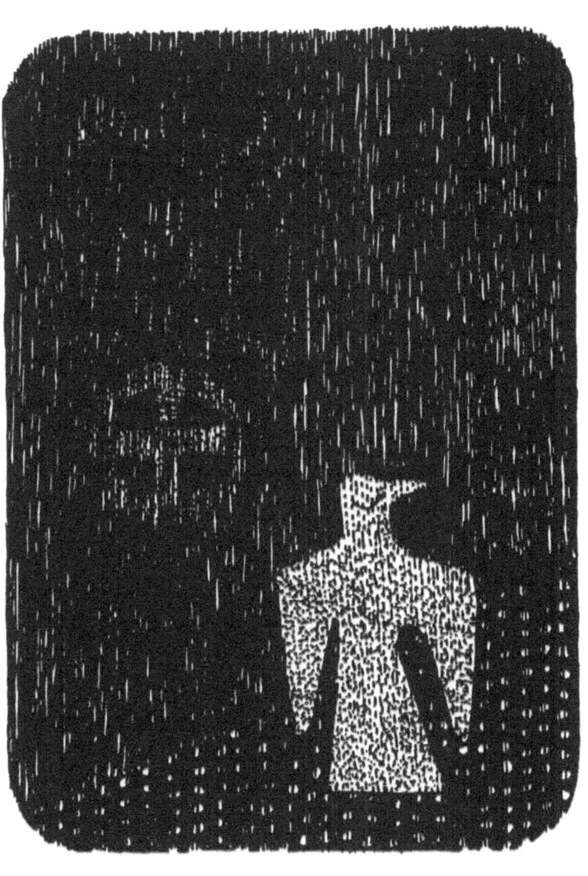

When Birch Leaves . . .

As if heaven were a white rose drooping,
Drooping down, the petals fall, not petals exactly
And not exactly white, snowing us.

The birch leaves fall, seeming to be white
In an atmosphere of white which they themselves
Pretend. They pretend spring is a dainty bell that

Only leaves can ring, their silent swirls describing
Sound. Gently, gently we are rung and gently we
Awake, singing not beauty seen, but beauty felt.

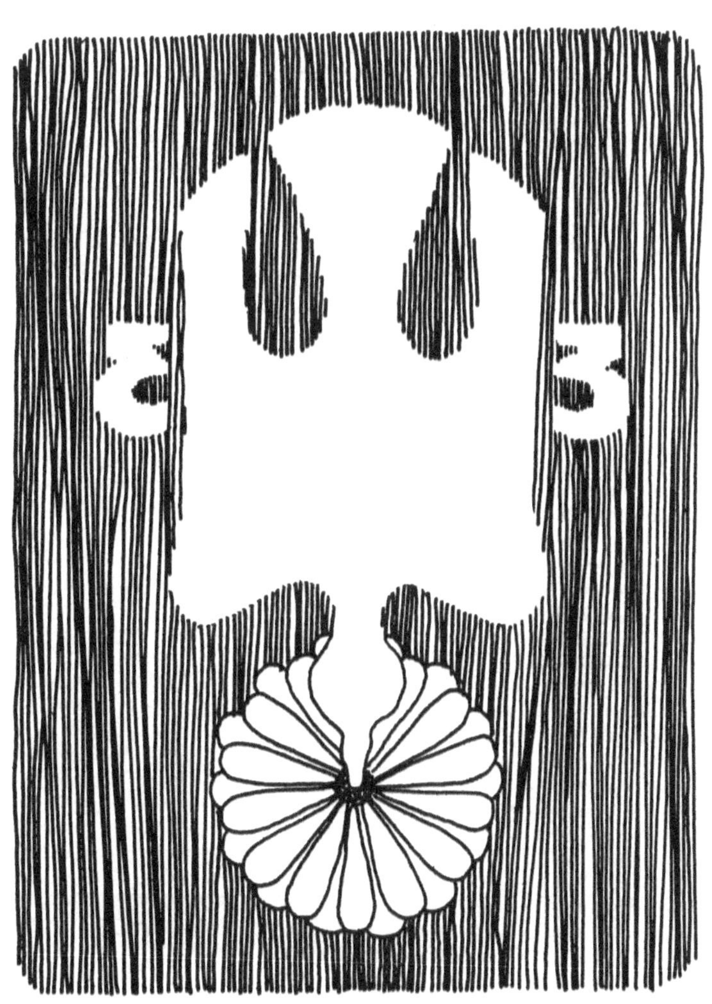

Genesis

Celebrate the hills with wildflowers,
Call out violet. yellow. red.
Let the new grass gentle the shoulders
Of the mountain and lead the wind

Down, down, softly down to the sea.
Then will the sun tumble in the waves,
And the leaves of a thousand trees
Shiver with joy.

Then will the light hold color and movement;
And the color, perfume.
Hear, o hear, all peoples,
How the universe pronounces your glorious name!

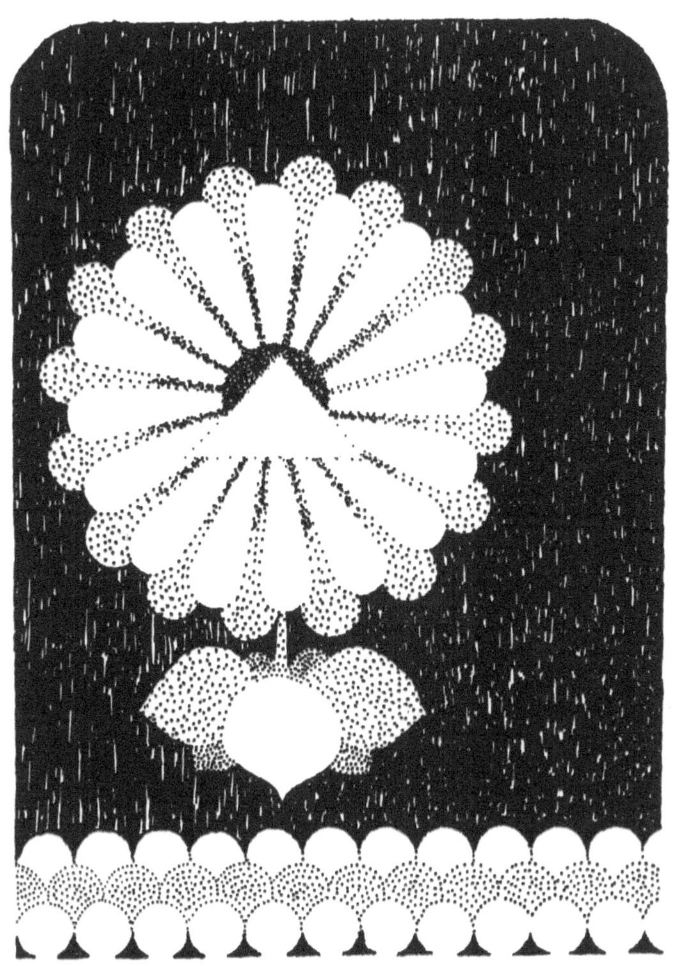

A Freedom Of The Mind

I left myself behind on the highway,
Left myself loose-jointedly flapping on the line there
By the redwood cabin as someone's pale blue shirt.

Whoosh! I am the freest thing in all these redwood
Mountains, with wind my only body, with sun
My body, a pale blue light leaping under trees.

Where is a bird who can mimic the sky's
Blue billows the way I can? What sedately
Winging wren guffaws in flight like this? Ha,

Bodiless blue! I am the freest thing in all
These redwood mountains.

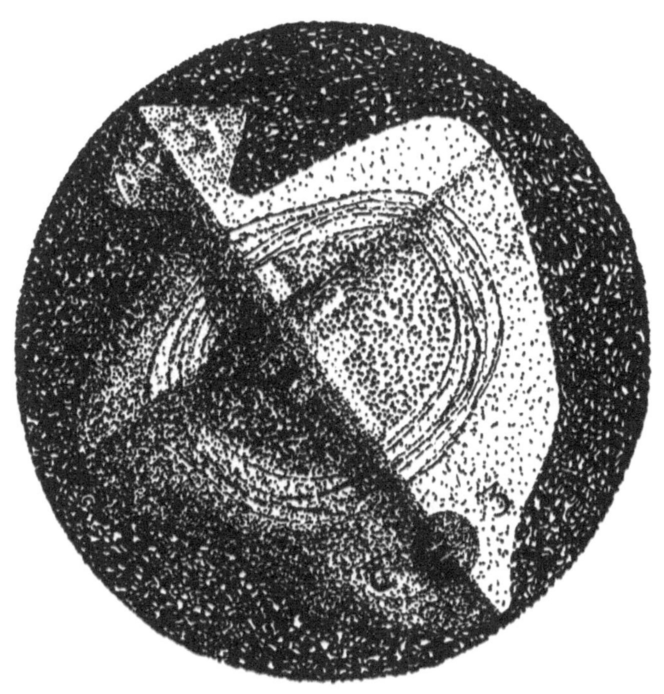

A Butterfly Is Itself

Some days love seems to be
A white butterfly
Visiting a white-blossomed bush.

It is like a white blossom itself,
Trembling there,
And the flowers we liken to
Delicate smiles from the moon.

And the moon - - -
The moon is like the spirit-wings
Of the butterfly that lives forever,
Whose heart is a glowing world of stars,

Who is a universe,
And graces us with light.

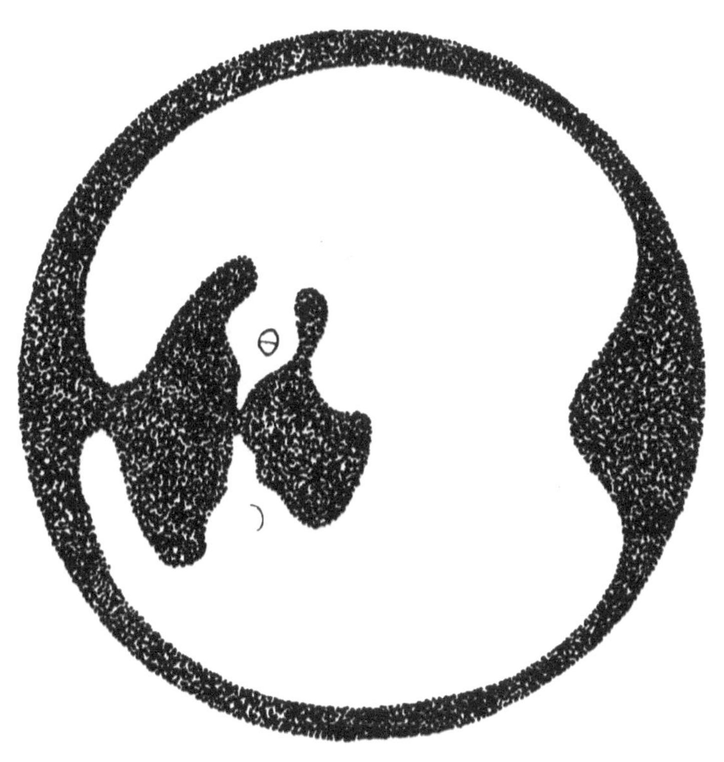

A Child's Offering Of Dandelions

This flower is my love:
Not formed by me, or willed - - -
And yet it grew, clarioned in the grass,
Smiled,

'Take me. Offer me in the sun.
Be free, for in my place whole
Fields shall spring to bloom.'

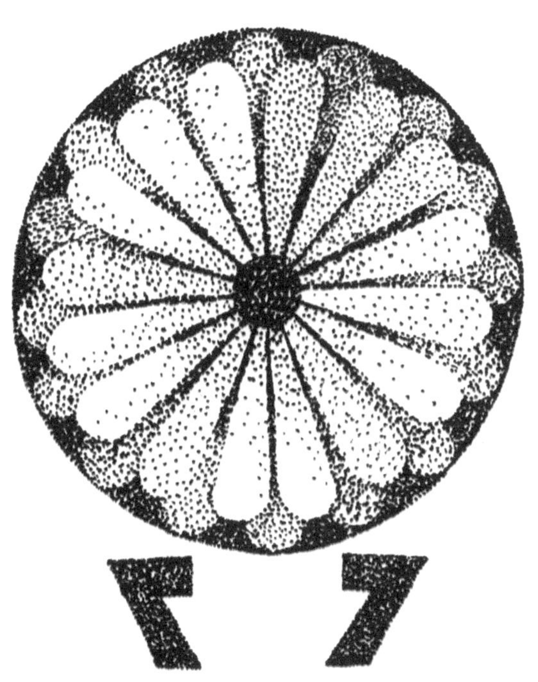

For Carol the Invisible

When the wind rippled you
On the hill and you stood
Streaming back with the tall blond grass,
A fluid being in a world made fluid
By the wind,

I knew that by some alchemy of the sun
You were as gold and as invisible
As the grass, and in that golden center
Held the world.

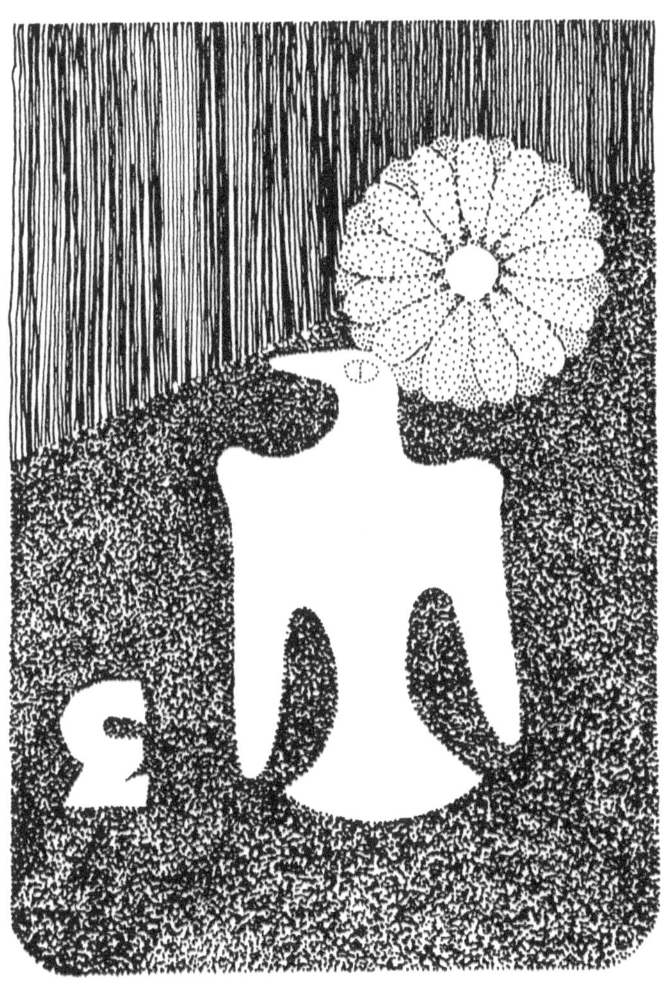

For A Prisoner

Your garden has walls for the sun to climb,
And the full moon catches in your trees. . .
And though you have enclosed all loveliness,
Beauty sleeps somewhere beneath the leaves,

And liberates the planets for the world,
And, invisibly, endows your garden
With an immensity you could not guess
Until some morning touched you

With its early light, and you
Walked out to find the sun belonged
To everyone, and that your home
Was vaster than the mind.

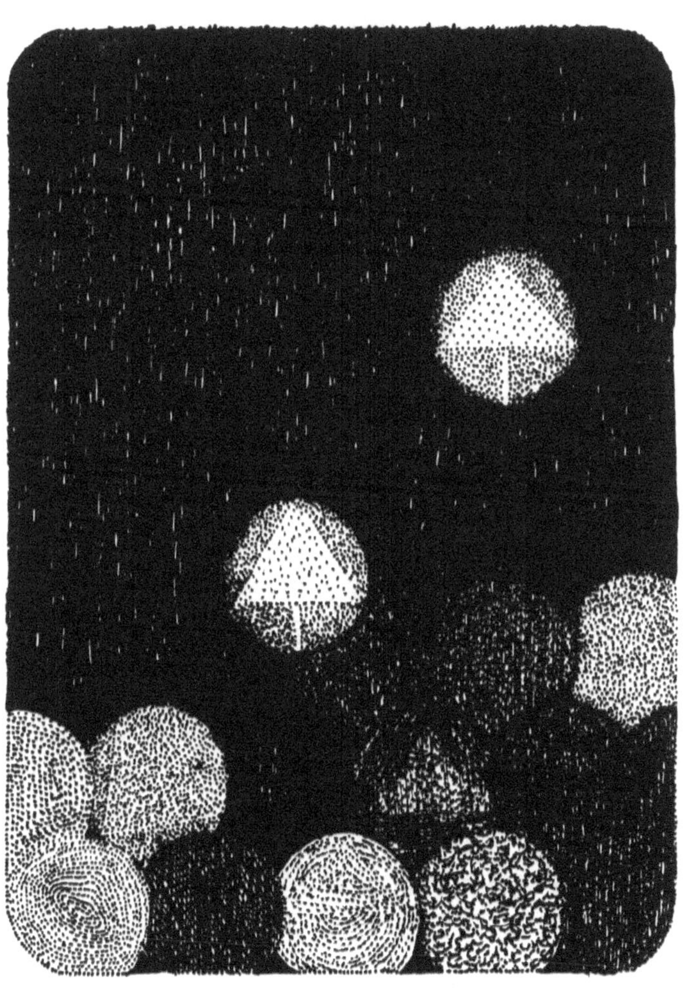

To Include All Things

Part I. Becoming the things we love

He knew the mountain was a god and that the clouds
Were white doves hovering, the god's feather mantle
And his sound;

And once in a botanical garden he heard
The laughter of something great, echoing in
Red hibiscus, in gay grotesqueries of trees.

Ah day of shadowy perceptions: he felt
His mountain shoulders meet the rain, saw
Godly hibiscus growing in his soul, and

Wonderingly, wondrously, entered a cloud.

II. 'I will give you the morning star.'

At night the city was a dragon with topaz eyes,
Burning the mind. It roared with carnival bravado
To reassure itself of life - - - and we walked on

In silence like the sky, including all things.
We walked, including the dragon and his ugly
Eye, including his beautiful topaz eye

As if we were impersonal galaxies - - as if
The promise had been fulfilled, and we
Were given the morning star.

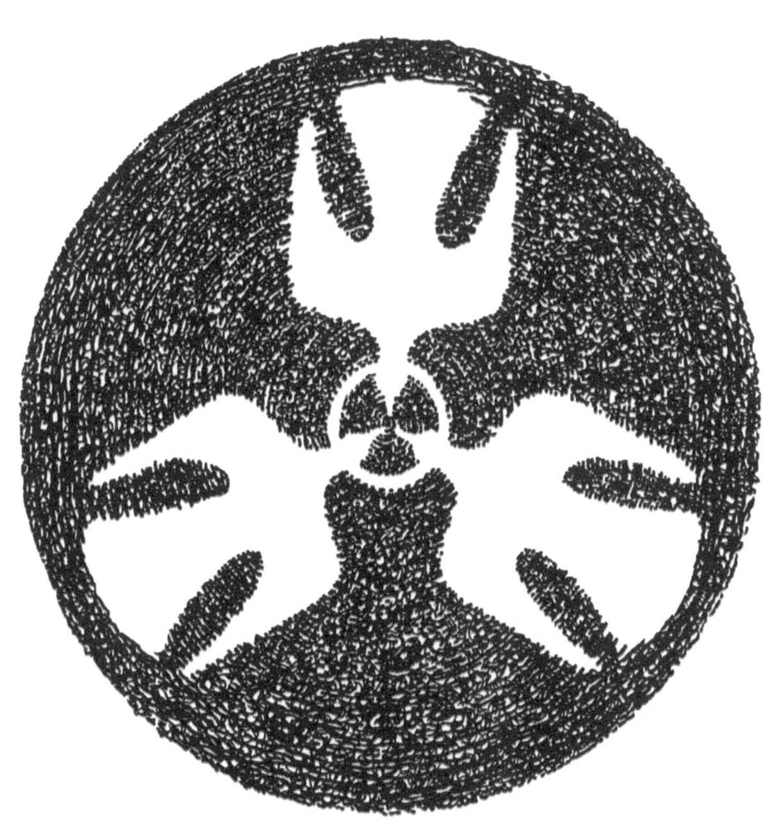

A Question Containing Its Own Answer

If I fell like this leaf to the ground
And lay in deepest shadow on the earth

Would you come with the sun to find me,
Would you come to that most hidden place

And illumine all that had lain down to die
In the grass, would this dullness glow once

Again, and would you touch me with the radiance
Of a thousand rosy mornings,

As you did this leaf?

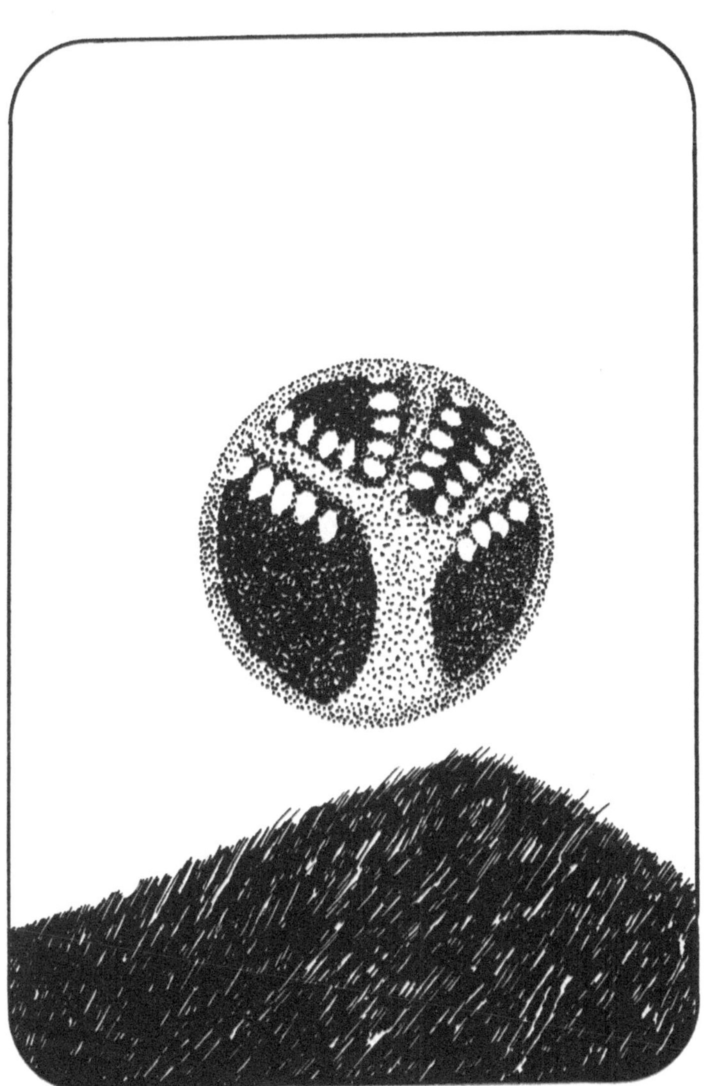

Some days we are empty fields
The wind crosses quickly to forget.

The sun never moves; and over the grass
The slow shadow of a crow is always the same.

We can only wait for eternity to cross over
Like the wind. We can only wait,

Dry grass standing, for a signal
Deep in the earth, for the promise of rain.

Some day (it has happened before)
We will be fields for harvesting.

Some day, out of emptiness,
A voice like life sweeps over the land.

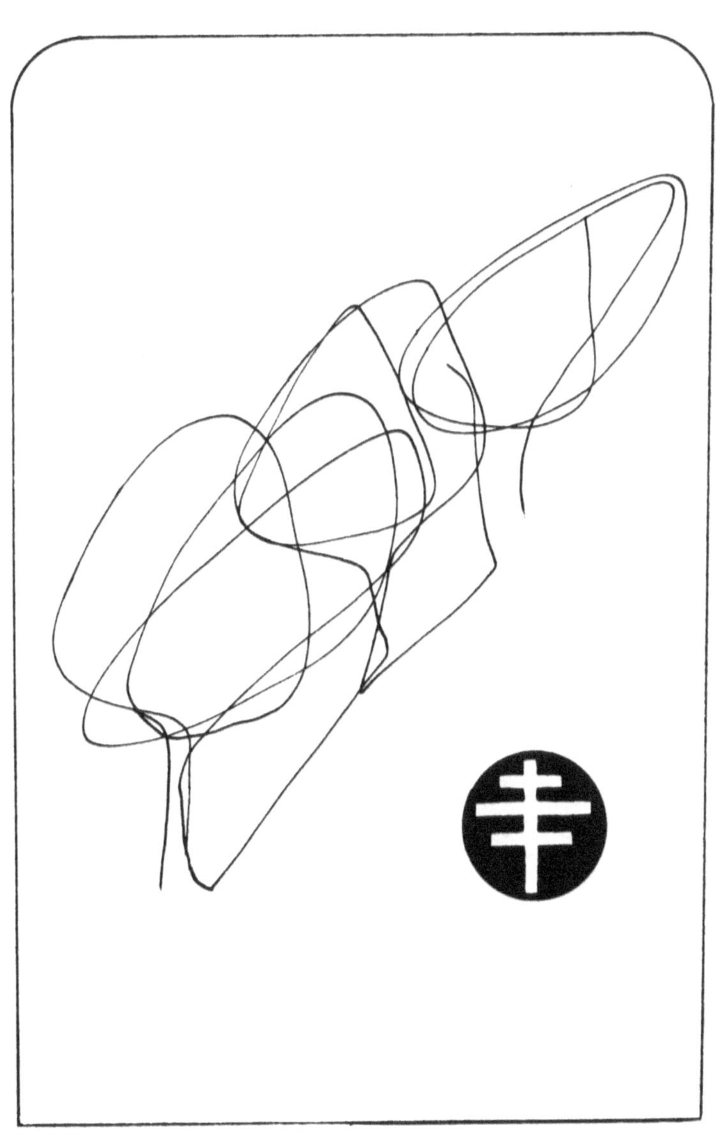

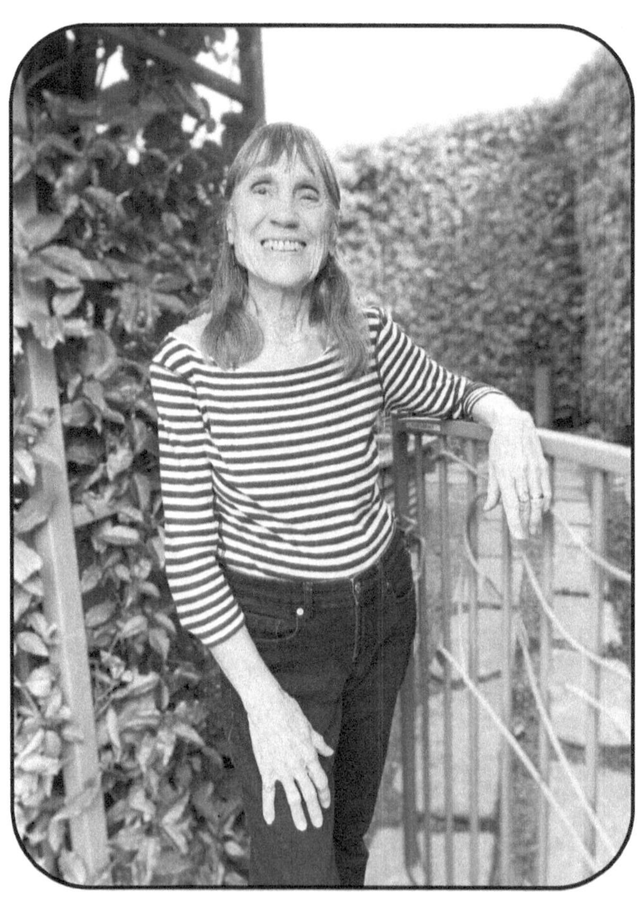

Photography by Cindy Fitzgerald ©2024

ABOUT THE AUTHOR

Joyce Winslow is an artist and writer in Eugene, Oregon. Her poetry has been published in the *Northwest Poets and Artists Calendar* and the *Northwest Review's Anthology of Eugene Writers*. She has published feature articles in various newspapers and periodicals including *Southwest Art Magazine, Ceramics Monthly, The Willamette Valley Observer,* and the University of Oregon's monthly *IT Connection.*

Winslow studied painting and design at the Otis Art Institute in Los Angeles and developed her silkscreen technique under the mentorship of noted serigrapher Guy MacCoy, who is credited with first introducing silkscreen as an art form in the 1930s. Her work was exhibited in one-person shows in Germany at the Gallery L. Saussele in Bietigheim-Bissingen and the University of Stuttgart in the 1980s. Winslow was a charter member of the Northwest Print Council, which included her prints in traveling exhibitions throughout the U.S. and around the world. Her work is reviewed in the 1989 edition of the *California Art Review* and in the 1990 edition of *American Artists, An Illustrated Survey of Leading Contemporaries.* She is included in the archives of the National Museum of Women in the Arts in Washington, D.C.

More of her poetry and artwork can be seen at
www.joycewinslowart.com